Growing Readers

New Hanover County Public Library

Purchased with
New Hanover County Partnership for Children
and Smart Start Funds

Flag Day

by Mari C. Schuh

Consulting Editor: Gail Saunders-Smith, Ph.D.

Consultant: Alan Walden
Member, Executive Committee
National Flag Day Foundation

Pebble Books

an imprint of Capstone Press
Mankato, Minnesota

Pebble Books are published by Capstone Press
151 Good Counsel Drive, P.O. Box 669, Mankato, Minnesota 56002
http://www.capstone-press.com

1 2 3 4 5 6 08 07 06 05 04 03

Library of Congress Cataloging-in-Publication Data
Schuh, Mari C., 1975–
    Flag Day / by Mari C. Schuh.
    p. cm.—(National holidays)
    Summary: An introduction to the history, purpose, and observance of Flag Day,
when we honor our country's flag.
    Includes bibliographical references and index.
    ISBN 0-7368-1652-6 (hardcover)
    1. Flag Day—Juvenile literature. [1. Flag Day. 2. Holidays.] I. Title. II. Series.
JK1761.S38   2003
394.263—dc21   2002009675

Note to Parents and Teachers

The National Holidays series supports national social studies
standards related to understanding events that celebrate the
values and principles of American democracy. This book describes
and illustrates Flag Day. The photographs support early readers in
understanding the text. This book also introduces early readers to
subject-specific vocabulary words, which are defined in the Words
to Know section. Early readers may need assistance to read some
words and to use the Table of Contents, Words to Know, Read
More, Internet Sites, and Index/Word List sections of the book.

Table of Contents

June

S	M	T	W	T	F	S
1	2	3	4	5	6	7
8	9	10	11	12	13	14
15	16	17	18	19	20	21
22	23	24	25	26	27	28
29	30					

4

Flag Day is a holiday
in the United States.
It is on June 14.

Flag Day honors the flag of the United States.

The American flag
is sometimes called
the Stars and Stripes.
It is also called Old Glory.

In 1949, President
Harry Truman named
June 14 as Flag Day.

Some students learn about Flag Day in school. They study the history of the American flag.

People hang flags at their homes and businesses on Flag Day.

People celebrate Flag Day with parades and songs. They listen to speeches about American history.

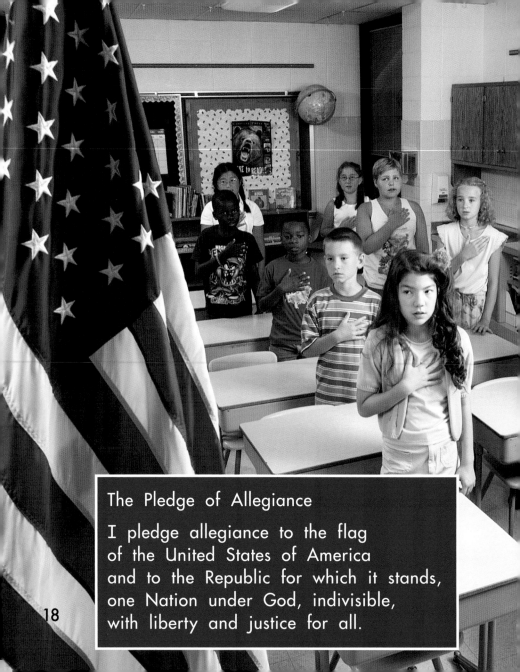

The Pledge of Allegiance

I pledge allegiance to the flag
of the United States of America
and to the Republic for which it stands,
one Nation under God, indivisible,
with liberty and justice for all.

People salute the flag on Flag Day. Some people say the Pledge of Allegiance.

Flag Day is a
day to respect
the American flag.

Words to Know

celebrate—to do something special on a certain day or week

flag—a cloth with a pattern that is a symbol of a country

history—events that happened in the past

honor—to show respect or to praise

parade—a line of people, bands, cars, and floats that travels through a town; parades celebrate special events and holidays.

Pledge of Allegiance—a promise to be loyal to the United States and its flag

respect—to admire or have a good opinion of something or someone

salute—to give a sign of respect

United States—a large country in North America; the United States has 50 states; the American flag has 50 stars.

Read More

Ansary, Mir Tamim. *Flag Day.* Holiday Histories.
Chicago: Heinemann Library, 2002.

Cooper, Jason. *Flag Day.* Holiday Celebrations.
Vero Beach, Fla.: Rourke Publishing, 2002.

Frost, Helen. *Independence Day.* National Holidays.
Mankato, Minn.: Pebble Books, 2000.

Raatma, Lucia. *Patriotism.* Character Education.
Mankato, Minn.: Bridgestone Books, 2000.

Internet Sites

Track down many sites about Flag Day.
Visit the FACT HOUND at *http://www.facthound.com*

IT IS EASY! IT IS FUN!

1) Go to *http://www.facthound.com*

2) Type in: 0736816526

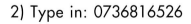

3) Click on "FETCH IT" and FACT HOUND will find
   several links hand-picked by our editors.

Index/Word List

Word Count: 116
Early-Intervention Level: 12

Credits
Heather Kindseth, series designer; Molly Nei, book designer; Gene Bentdahl,
illustrator; Karrey Tweten, photo researcher

Capstone Press/Nancy White, 1; Gary Sundermeyer, cover, 4, 8, 12, 14, 18
Corbis/Mug Shots, 6; Corbis/Bettman, 10; Corbis, 16
Index Stock Imagery/Danny Daniels, 20